McCrary Sisters
♥
Cooking with Love

Copyright © 2015 McCrary Sisters Productions, LLC
Cover photo: Padrion Scott
THE HOLY BIBLE, NEW INTERNATIONAL VERSION®, NIV®
Copyright © 1973, 1978, 1984, 2011 by Biblica, Inc.™ Used by permission.
All rights reserved.
ISBN: 0692568069
ISBN-13: 978-0692568064

Mamie Elizabeth Marsh McCrary

MUDEAR

Dedicated to Mudear

This cookbook is dedicated to the memory of our mother, Mamie Elizabeth (Marsh) McCrary. Our mother passed away on July 15, 1998. Mudear, as we all called her, was the best cook in the world because she cooked with love. She had passion for cooking. Whenever she wanted to show love, she cooked for us, and it was also her way to say she was sorry. People would hire her to cook a whole meal for them and they would come and pick it up. We would tell her that these people were going to take the meal home and take credit for preparing it, but she didn't care. She would only cook for people whom she cared for and it made her happy.

As soon as we walked in the front door, the smells would fill up our nostrils and our stomachs would growl in anticipation of the flavors that would roll across our tongues. Our mother would just make up recipes. Whatever was in her fridge or cabinets, she would throw together and make the best meal.

Mudear worked two jobs. Her first was as a cook in a public school cafeteria. We were told that when she became the head cook, not very many students would bring their own lunch to school. They preferred her cooking. Her second job was cleaning up an office building. She would come home from her first job, cook for us, and then go to her second job. Sometimes she would take food to her second job to feed the people that worked in the offices. These people loved the food, but most of all, they loved her.

In her later years, Mudear had to have her leg amputated as a result of being diabetic. She was the strongest woman I have ever known. As soon as she came home from the rehab, she got in her wheelchair and went straight to the kitchen. We would have to gather the ingredients for her and she proceeded to prepare the best meal ever. Even though she had to give up her two jobs, she never missed preparing a meal at home. When a surgery damaged a nerve in her arm and she did not have full use of her hand, she still cooked and showed her love.

Our first Thanksgiving without her should have been very painful, but it turned out to be a most joyful day. As each one of us prepared food to bring to our mother's house for the Thanksgiving feast, we each told the same story while preparing our dishes. We could feel our mother telling us what ingredients to add, and giving us step-by-step instructions. Then the table was set, the food was ready to eat and the prayer was said. One by one as each dish was sampled a wave of excitement came over us. Someone would say "who made this" or "who made that" because each dish would taste just like Mudear's. We were all so happy because it seemed as if she was still sitting in her recliner in the living room, listening and laughing at all of our stories.

It is still the same today. As I cook, I think of Mudear. *What would she add to this dish*, and to us, food is great when it tastes like Mudear's food. That's when you know it was cooked with love.

-Ann McCrary

Contents

Foreword 10
Mudear's Story 11
Cook to Your Taste and Appetite 12
House to House 13

Ann's House 14

Ann's Story 15
Ann's Egg Noodle Lasagna 16
Ann's Skillet Greens 18
Regina's Big Ole Salad 19
Freda's Hot Wings 20
Deborah's Spinach Dip 21
Mother Frankie's Peach Cobbler 22
Ann's 15 Bean Soup Plus 24

Regina's House 26

Regina's Story: Loving Memories of Mudear 27
Freda's Spiced Salmon 28
Regina's Spaghetti 29
Deborah's Spicy Slaw 30
Ann's Baked Potatoes 31
Regina's Fish Tacos 32
Regina's First Dish…Baked Beans 33
Regina's Key Lime Pie 35
Regina's Story: She Still Loved Me… 36

Regina's Birthday Bash Seafood Boil 37

Gina Mac Ooo Wee Seafood Gumbo 38

Regina's Steak & Potato Soup on a Cold Day 40

Regina's Creamy Chicken Vegetable Soup 42

Regina's Story: New Year Eve Wild Meat Dinner 44

Regina's Butt Pork Roast 45

Regina's Story: A Bag for the Road Full of Love 46

Regina's Quickie Hot Stuff 47

Regina's Healthy Quickie 48

Regina's Bologna Sammich 49

Regina's Story: If There's a Kitchen in Heaven 50

Freda's House 51

Freda's Story 52

Freda's Pot Pie 53

Ann's Ground Beef & Turkey Meatloaf 54

Regina's Potatoes & Onions 55

Ann's Hot Water Cornbread 56

Deborah's Hot Water Cornbread 57

Regina's Hmmm Good Caramel Pie 58

Freda's Party Dip 59

Freda's Tomato Artichoke Salad 60

Deborah's House 61

Deborah's Story 62

Deborah's Baked Chicken 63

Deborah's Fried Cabbage 64

Freda's Fried Corn 65

Ann's Mashed Potatoes (with Cheese and/or Broccoli) 66

Regina's Green Beans—Watch Out Now! 67

Tommy & Becky's Peanut Butter Pie 68

Deborah's Story: Play Cookin' to the Real Cookin' 69

Sundays at the McCrary's 70

Regina's Story: Funny Sunday Morning Memory 71

Regina's Fried Apples 72

Ann's Pork Chops & Gravy 73

Holidays at the McCrary's 74

Regina's Holiday Story 75

Regina's Ham for Christmas 76

McCrary Holiday Turkey & Dressing 77

Cisco's Country Skillet Bread 78

Eben & Cathy's Cornbread Dressing 79

Ann's Potato Salad 80

Ann's Pineapple Sweet Potatoes 81

Ann's Stuffed Eggs 83

Deborah's Cheesy Macaroni & Cheese 84

Freda's Collard Greens 85

Ann's Corn Pudding 87

Ann's Baked Cherry Cheese Pie 88

Ann's Chess Pie 89

Cathy's Fudge 90

McCrary Cooking and Table Do's and Don'ts 92

Foreword

The stories and recipes written by the McCrary Sisters, Ann, Deborah, Regina and Freda, are shared with love. Love for their mother who was known as Mudear, to whom this book is dedicated, and love for their own individual families. I know firsthand what it's like to share food made with love by the Sisters. One of my earliest experiences was visiting them at a recording studio and from the moment I walked in, they were trying to feed you. Regina walked me back to the kitchen area and spooned up a large, wonderful dish of her homemade chicken soup and it was so good. Good, flavorful and healthy.

The McCrary Sisters are four in a group of eight siblings raised in Nashville by their mother and father, the Reverend Samuel McCrary, one of the founders of the Fairfield Four. The girls were raised in harmony singing together from the time they were very little, but they were also raised in a house full of the wonderful smells of some of the recipes you'll find in this book.

I sat with the sisters one day in the very same dining room where they ate Mudear's famous cooking and Ann McCrary told me her Daddy said Mudear wasn't always a great cook. She learned how to become a great cook and she passed this skill on to the Sisters who are sharing their recipes with you, with love.

-**Joan Williams**

Mudear's Story

Mudear was born as Mamie Elizabeth Marsh in Bell Buckle, TN, on December 3, 1924, and passed away July 15, 1998, in Nashville. She was 1 of 16 children. There were four sets of twins among these siblings. Out of all the siblings, only one is still living, Mildred Ruth Jackson.

We were told that their parents died when Mudear was young. So the oldest siblings raise the younger ones and when they would get married and leave, the younger ones would go with them.

Times were really hard in those days. There were times when there were no food in the house, and they would steal chickens from some of the farmers. Or in the winter months, they told of how they would chase the coal trains, and the older one would throw coal off the train and the younger one would fill their sacks and baskets up with coal, so they would have heat for the winter. Some things they wouldn't even talk about. I know life was hard.

Mudear wouldn't throw away any food. She would find a way to recycle it and it was always good. Her freezer stayed full all the time. Sometime the meat would get freezer burnt because it had been in the freezer too long. You could tell that she had issue of never being hungry again. And she never was.

Everyone thinks that the singing part of the family only came from the McCrary side, but the Marsh family were some singing folk. I was told that our grandfather Jesse Marsh was a great singer. So the singing came from both sides. Mudear never wanted to sing very much, but she could sing. She had a soprano voice. The only time we got to hear her sing was as a choir member of the Fairfield Baptist Church, or after my father became pastor of the St. Mark Missionary Baptist Church, he would convince her to sing every once in awhile, and for him she would reluctantly do it, and she would sing until the whole church was on fire. Wow we loved to hear her sing.

Daddy said that when they first got married, Mudear couldn't cook. But love for her family turned her cooking into an art. We love you Mudear.

-McCrary Sisters

Cook to Your Taste and Appetite

The one thing to remember about our recipes is most of our cooking is done by taste and not measurement. For new cooks we have added some measurements, but for seasoned cooks all you need are the ingredients and the rest is history.

House to House

During the year we will get together and bring food to each other's houses. It doesn't have to be a special occasion but because we like being around each other and we love to eat the food. These are times filled with love, and yes we do have disagreements, but the connection of love and family remains.

Ann's House

Ann's Story

Ann's Menu:

Ann's Egg Noodle Lasagna

Ann's Skillet Greens

Regina's Big Ole Salad

Freda's Hot Wings

Deborah's Spinach Dip

Mother Frankie's Peach Cobbler

Ann's Extra:

Ann's 15 Bean Soup Plus

Ann's Story

Mudear was very strict with her children, especially the girls. She wanted a better life for us than the one that she had. She wanted me to finish high school and go to college. It was always my intention to go to college, but I fooled around and fell in love.

Mudear did not like the guy I was with and she made no secret about it. (Of course later in life she loved him dearly.) She treating him so bad and he kept coming around. He finally went into the Air Force, and I went to college for a little while. But I finally had enough of her bad mouthing him, so I quit school, and ran away from home. I just knew that I had enough friends who would let me stay with them, and I didn't need my family anymore. So I ended up running from one person's house to another, and finding out that my friends were being nice, but after one or two days they were ready for you to go. I wanted to go home so bad, but I wanted Mudear to accept my choice.

The weather had started to get cold, and I needed to get a coat from home. So I waited for Sunday to come, because I knew Mudear would be at church. She never missed going to church unless she was sick. I went to the house and I found my coat, and as I turned the corner to leave my room Mudear was standing there. My heart started beating real fast and I just knew she was going to beat me down. So I braced myself, and when I looked up at her and into her eyes, she was crying and she threw her arms around me. And she said, "I'm sorry." I was almost in the state of shock because Mudear did not say I'm sorry. She asked me to come home, and said that I had the right to choose to love whomever I please.

I had so many mixed emotions. I was glad to be home, glad to mend my relationship with Mudear. But then I felt bad that I made her cry. But I didn't break her spirit, because with all of my sisters, she never liked any of their choices in men, and she let them know.

Most of the times she was right with her discernment about these guys. There was nobody like her.

Ann's Egg Noodle Lasagna

This is one of my special dishes. When I made this all of my children would eat all of their food. When I was married years ago, we lived in Italy and I love their food. It was such an art to make lasagna there, and I could never make it right, so I just gave up. Years later when I got back home, I made my first dish of noodle lasagna and it was a hit! I wish I could make the lasagna the way they make it in Italy, but this will do. My mother loved this recipe and it made my heart so happy to know that I cooked a dish of my own that she loved. This recipe is for a small to medium dish. For our big family, I have to double everything.

Ingredients

1 1/2 lb. ground beef
12 oz. bag of egg noodles
1 onion
1 package of dry spaghetti sauce
1 small can tomato paste
I medium can tomato sauce
1 tsp sugar
salt
black pepper
1 package shredded cheddar cheese
1 package mozzarella cheese
1 Tbsp cooking oil
1 small tub of cottage cheese
1 small tub of sour cream

Directions

In a large skillet, sauté the onion then add ground beef and season to taste. While ground beef is cooking, boil noodles.

Sauce
After ground beef is cooked, drain most of the excess oil off of the meat.
Add the dry spaghetti sauce and 1/2 cup of water then stir well.

Add tomato paste and 1 cup of water. Your sauce should not be dry, so use your judgment on using more water.

Add sugar and stir well. At this time, taste the sauce to determine if you should add any more seasoning, because you know better than anyone how your family taste buds are.

Put sauce on low heat and let it simmer for 15-20 minutes.

Pasta

After noodles are done cooking, drain the water.

Put the noodles in a mixing bowl and add cottage cheese and mix well, then add cream cheese and mix well. Once again use your judgment about using the cottage cheese or cream cheese. I use all of it.

After the sauce and the pasta is ready, in a medium baking dish layer 1/2 of pasta mix, then spoon 1/2 of sauce over the pasta.

Evenly spread 1/2 of cheddar cheese on top of that and then evenly spread 1/2 of mozzarella cheese on top.

Repeat the layers again with the mozzarella cheese on top.

Cook on 350° for 40-45 minutes. Ovens sometimes cook differently, so don't let the cheese get too brown or it will be too hard on top.

This should feed 6 people or more depending on much your guests like to eat. Enjoy!

Ann's Skillet Greens

I love greens, all kinds of greens. I don't ever want to get tired of eating greens, so sometimes I will think of different ways to cook them. Of course, kale and spinach are very good raw, and I love both of them. I have also had both kale and spinach sautéed and that is delicious. I decided to do something that was a little different and I loved it, and maybe you will too. I call this Skillet Greens.

Ingredients

1 lb. or a bunch of kale
1 lb. or a bunch of spinach
1 large onion
1 package sliced mushrooms (fresh are best)
1 Tbsp butter
olive oil
1 slice bacon for more flavor (optional)

Directions

In a large skillet, cover the bottom with olive oil.
Add butter and cut up bacon to skillet.
Thoroughly wash the kale (make sure you get all of the sand or dirt off).
Cut onion into small pieces.
Put the kale into the oil mixture in the skillet and put the cut onions on top of the kale.
Cover and cook over medium heat for 10 minutes.
While the kale is cooking, wash the spinach. After 10 minutes, stir the kale and onions then cook for another 5 minutes.
After 5 minutes, add mushrooms to the kale and onions, cover and cook for another 10 minutes.
Stir and add spinach into the mixture right away. Cook on medium-low heat for 10 to 15 minutes longer if you desire more tenderness.
In 40 minutes, you will have greens in a different way. Enjoy!
(Feeds 4-5 people)

Regina's Big Ole Salad

Ingredients

1 big bag of lettuce (your choice)
1 head of romaine lettuce (chopped)
1 bag or bunch of spinach
green olives
black olives
carrots (shredded or sliced)
beets (shredded or sliced)
mandarin orange segments
sunflower seeds
cheese (shredded or cubed)
bacon bits

Directions

Mix all the lettuce together in a big bowl.
Then put all of the ingredients in small bowls, so whatever you like you can add to your salad. Have all your dressing sitting out.

Freda's Hot Wings

Ingredients

1 package of wings
hot sauce
butter
salt
pepper

Directions

Thaw chicken.
Preheat oven to 350°.
Season wings with salt and pepper to taste.
Cook until done, about 45 minutes—soft or hard, your preference.
Melt butter and mix together with hot sauce.
Pour sauce over wings.

Deborah's Spinach Dip

My daughter LaToya was raised by me and my parents. We all lived with my parents. And she knows firsthand about the good cooking that Mudear did. This is LaToya's recipe for Spinach Dip. And it is so, so good.

Ingredients

4 boxes of chopped frozen spinach
2 eggs per box of spinach, or 8 eggs (beaten)
parmesan cheese
minced garlic
olive oil
Italian seasoning

Directions

In a large skillet, heat olive oil and then add minced garlic.
Add spinach to the pan.
After spinach cooks, add eggs and stir as they cook.
Add parmesan cheese and season to taste.

Mother Frankie's (Regina's friend) Peach Cobbler

I joined a church named Grace New Vision and I met a beautiful woman by the name of Mother Frankie (a.k.a. my play Mom). Oh my God, I love her so much! She's a very kind-hearted, spiritual woman of God.

Mother Frankie makes me smile. Her straight shootin', tell you like it is, reminds me of my Momma (Mudear). Then I tasted her cooking and I spiritually felt my Momma's spirit. Mother Frankie is my other mother, so I asked Mother Frankie if she would bless you guys with her famous peach cobbler, and she said yes! So hold on to your seat, this is gonna be great!

<u>**Filling**</u>

Ingredients

2 lbs. of fresh peaches (or apples — you can substitute 1 large can of peaches or apples)
1/2 tsp mace
1 tsp nutmeg
1/4 tsp cayenne pepper
2 tsp of vanilla
1 stick of butter (melted)
3 cups of sugar (less or more, to your taste)

Directions

Mix all of the ingredients together and put the mixture into a piecrust (fresh or store bought).

Pie Crust

Ingredients

2 cups plain flour
3/4 tsp of salt
2/3 cups butter
1/3 cup of water (cold)

Directions

Preheat oven to 350°.
Blend butter, salt and flour together.
After mixing all together, add the cold water and work it all together with your hands.
Roll out to make the piecrust (it will fill a 9-inch pan) and save a few strips for the top of the cobbler, or fold over to top the filling.
Lay the crust on the bottom of the pan
Put peaches (or apple) mixture in to the crust, making sure the peaches are inside of the crust.
Brush butter on top of crust and sprinkle some sugar on top of the crust.
Placing into the warm oven and bake for one hour or until golden brown.

Ann's 15 Bean Soup Plus

Whenever the weather started to get cold, we knew that Mudear would be making soup to warm our bodies. She could make soup out of anything. She would throw stuff together and make up names for it. When we would say, "This is so good, what is it?" She would say, "Pi pussy pie," or "Puss," or anything that came to her mind.

Mudear was a cut up, and what came up, came out. I took her to a church picnic, and I set our table far from the pastor or the deacon's table, because I knew she was going to cut up. She was so funny. Well wouldn't you know that one of the mothers of the church set her table right next to ours. Then a friend of mine who knew that my mom would, came to our table and she was encouraging Mudear to cut up. My daughter and son-in-law came to our table. We had the best time trying to hide Mudear's cussing and bad talking from some of those church folk. As for everyone who knew her, and loved her, we had a good time eating the food that she fixed, and laughing.

If you didn't want to know the truth about yourself or the situation you were living in, then it was best not to go around Mudear, because she was going to tell you whether you wanted to hear it or not. I may not have wanted to hear her words then, but I sure do wish I could hear them now.

Back to the soups. I'm sure you will love it.

Ingredients

1 lb. bag 15 beans
1 small chicken or hen
bacon, smoked turkey or olive oil
1 large onion
salt
black pepper
1 lb. bag kale
1 can Rotel tomatoes
seasoning salt

Directions

The night before cooking, clean and soak beans overnight.
Boiled chicken or hen until very tender (hens will take much longer to cook).
Put beans in a large pot.
Add enough of your bacon, turkey or oil for seasoning.
Add onion, salt, pepper and seasoning salt.
Fill the pot with water, almost to the top.
Cook on medium high for 30 minutes.
Reduce heat to medium and cook another hour.
While your beans are cooking, wash and drain the kale.
After an hour and a half, add your kale the beans.
Make sure you have enough water in the pot. The soup should start to have a little thickness to it.
Add Rotel tomatoes.
Cook bean mixture for another 30 to 45 minutes.
Your chicken should be ready to peel off the bone, so cut your chicken to your desired size.
Add 1 1/2 cups of chicken broth to bean mixture.
Stir chicken into bean mixture.
Let it cook for another 30 minutes.
If the bean mixture starts to get too thick, add more broth.
Season to desired taste, and enjoy. This dish would be very good with cornbread. And if you don't eat meat, it is also delicious without the chicken.

Regina's House

Regina's Story

Regina's Menu:

Freda's Spiced Salmon

Regina's Spaghetti

Deborah's Spicy Slaw

Ann's Baked Potatoes

Regina's Fish Tacos

Regina's Baked Beans

Regina's Key Lime Pie

Regina's Extras:

Regina's Story: She Still Loved Me…

Regina's Birthday Bash Seafood Boil

Gina Mac Ooo Wee Seafood Gumbo

Regina's Steak and Potato Soup on a Cold Day

Regina's Creamy Chicken Vegetable Soup

Regina's Story: New Year Eve Wild Meat Dinner

Regina's Butt Pork Roast

Regina's Story: A Bag for the Road Full of Love

Regina's "Quickie" Hot Stuff

Regina's Healthy Quickie

Regina's Bologna Sammich

Regina's Story: If There's a Kitchen in Heaven

Regina's Story: Loving Memories of Mudear

(I love you)

This is a salute to Mudear (my momma). I love her so much. She not only was a gifted and talented mom, wife, sister, aunt, friend, she was a dancer...yes, dancer. Lord, my momma could dance. Whatever new dance was out for the young people (at that time me), she would watch us do the latest dance, then look at us and say, "Y'all ain't doin' nothing. That's an old dance. We did that dance when I was younger." And Mudear could cut a rug (an old saying for dancing good). Mudear could do that dance just as great as we did, if not greater.

Mudear was beautiful—her smile, her big eyes, gorgeous brown smooth skin—and she was kind, loving and she had a wonderful heart. And fun. But Mudear didn't and wouldn't take nothing off of anybody. Mudear would feed you and cuss you out. She only did that to people she loved. She even cussed out Bob Dylan when he came to our home to have dinner with my family. Mudear told him to come to the kitchen where she was because she needed to make sure he was eating. Then she looked at him and said, "I gotta make you eat with your skinny ass," and Bob laughed. Mudear put her arms around Bob, sat him down and fed him, and man, did he eat. And he took a plate with him. Off and on Bob sometimes mentions that night with a smile on his face. And he loved my mother's cooking...he loved my mom.

Well, in our home when it came to Mudear's cooking, I've seen so many people come to eat Mudear's cooking—L. Maria Muldaur, Reverend James Cleveland, Fairfield Four, Dorothy Love Coates, Staple Singers, Reverend Joe Mayes and many more. All these people, plus St. Mark's Baptist Church where my Daddy pastored until he passed. Mudear's cooking was...no, is legendary. I'm so glad she taught me everything I know... I love you.

Freda's Spiced Salmon

When Mudear taught us how to cook, we didn't do a lot of measuring. As you read some of these recipes, it's really taste as you go, if that makes sense. Just judge the amount you use and do a little different a little at a time.

I hope and pray that this book of our recipes will be a help and a blessing for some. This was done out of love. Thank you.

Ingredients

salmon (fresh is preferred)
seafood seasoning or seasoning salt
2 Tbsp butter
garlic cloves (chopped)
juice of 1/2 lemon

Directions

Preheat a pan.
Season the salmon on both sides.
Place 2 Tbsp of butter in pan and cook salmon for seven minutes, turning one time.
Add chopped garlic and lemon juice and cook for two more minutes.
Or you can cook the garlic, lemon juice and butter separately and pour over the salmon.
Enjoy!

Regina's Spaghetti (This is so special!)

My son's name is Tony, and Tony and I both love spaghetti. I would make a pot of spaghetti just for him. It's not that I had a wonderful recipe for spaghetti, but if I had a pot of spaghetti on the stove, Tony would eat and eat. Spaghetti would even win out over Fruit Loops. Tony would rather eat Fruit Loops than breakfast, lunch or dinner. But when I made that spaghetti…wow!
I remember hearing Tony say, "Hey Momma, will you make me some spaghetti?" I'm gonna share this with you and hey, it had to be pretty good if it could beat out Fruit Loops. I love and miss cooking spaghetti for you Tony…love Momma!

Ingredients

1 or 2 cans of spaghetti sauce
2-3 lbs. of ground beef
1 box spaghetti noodles
1 whole onion
1 whole bell pepper
minced garlic (fresh or crushed)
salt
black pepper
2 Tbsp sugar

Directions

In a skillet, cook and brown the ground beef. Cut up the bell pepper and onion then cook them both with the ground beef.
When browned, pour excess grease off of the beef.
While cooking the ground beef, onions and bell pepper, boil the spaghetti noodles in a large pot of water. Pour a small amount of olive oil in water and as it boils, add the noodles.
When spaghetti noodles are ready, pour water off and let it set for two minutes.
Then pour the ground beef mixture, salt, pepper and minced garlic (to taste), all together into the pot.
Open up a can of spaghetti sauce and put into the pot, mixing it all together.
Reduce heat to medium on the stove (level 5) and let cook for 10 minutes, and then reduce heat to low. Then eat, eat, eat!

Deborah's Spicy Slaw

Ingredients

1 cabbage
1 green pepper
mustard
mayo
sugar
black pepper

Directions

Combine cut up cabbage and green pepper in a large bowl.
Add mayo, sugar, mustard and black pepper.
Stir ingredients and taste.

Ann's Baked Potatoes

Everyone should know how to bake a potato.

Ingredients

potatoes
butter
salt
pepper

Directions

If you are using a conventional oven, preheat to 400°. Rub a little butter on the skin of the potato and cook for 45 minutes.

If you want to microwave your potato, check to see if your microwave has a setting for baked potatoes. If there is no setting, cook from 5-10 minutes depending on the size of the potato. Season and eat to your heart's desire.

Regina's Fish Tacos

Ingredients

taco shells
tilapia fish
lettuce
onion (if you like)
cheese
taco sauce (your choice)
butter
olive oil
salt
garlic powder
cayenne pepper
sour cream

Directions

Take skillet and cut heat on high.
Put olive oil and butter in skillet.
When it all melts, place tilapia into skillet.
Cook, cut it up into pieces and take out of skillet.
Put it in a bowl so you can make your fish taco.
Place fish at bottom of taco shell, then cheese, then lettuce, taco sauce and sour cream.

Regina's First Dish...Baked Beans

Okay, I think I was the daughter that ran from the kitchen. Maybe I would have liked it as a little girl, but with 8 kids, 4 boys and 4 girls, plus our parents—10 people! We would take turns cleaning the kitchen. Everyone had a week long to clean the kitchen...yeah, you had seven weeks off, but man it felt like when it was my week, my momma would cook all the foods that would stick to the pots and pans.

I hated the kitchen, so when Mudear would call me into the kitchen to teach me to cook, I would act so dumb. I would just say, "I don't understand." Mudear would get so mad at me and tell me to get out of her kitchen and I would run. Well, I would act like I was sad, but truly I was happy.

When Mudear started to cook her baked beans, I would still act dumb, but I watched everything she did, everything she put in her beans. So one day when I was older, I didn't want Mudear to feel like she had failed at teaching me how to cook. On the Fourth of July, when we had our biggest family cookout, I told everybody including my Mom I would make the baked beans. Everybody got quiet, looked at each other. Mudear said, "Are you sure?" I said, "Yes," with a smile.

Well let me just say, Mudear was so proud, and I've been making the baked beans ever since that day. See Mudear, I did pay attention. I love you...thank you!

Ingredients

1 or 2 large cans baked beans
1 1/2 cups brown sugar
1/2 cup regular sugar
2 bottles of barbeque sauce
2 nice sized onions
2 green bell peppers
5 lbs. ground beef (or more)
salt
black pepper

Directions

Cook your ground beef in a skillet. Chop your onion and bell pepper up and put into the ground beef as it cooks. Let it all cook together.

Take your 1 or 2 large cans of baked beans and pour into a large pot.

Take the brown sugar, sugar and barbeque sauce then pour it all in with the beans.

Drain the grease off of the ground beef, and then pour the ground beef/onion/green pepper mixture into the pot.

Add the pinch of salt and pepper.

Stir, mixing it all together.

Put on medium heat (level 6) on top of the stove for about 20-30 minutes, then put on low heat until you are ready to eat.

Regina's Key Lime Pie

Ingredients

2 cans of condensed milk
3 limes
Cool Whip
graham cracker piecrust

Directions

Preheat oven to 350°.
Pour two cans of condensed milk in small saucepan.
Squeeze lime juice and stir into milk.
Cook on medium high for 5 minutes.
Pour mixture into piecrust.
Put pie in oven for 30 minutes.
After 30 minutes, cut off oven, take out pie and let it cool. Your choice to eat warm or cold. Chill pie if you want it cold.
Then squeeze a few drops of lime in Cool Whip, spread on pie and serve…hmmm.

Regina's Story: She Still Loved Me...

At the age of 17 years old I got pregnant. I hid it for as long as I could but when Mudear finally found out I was pregnant she cried so pitifully and she was hurt and disappointed. I'm her seventh child out of eight and my daddy the pastor of St. Mark's Church. Well I was so ashamed and I know I disappointed them to be 17 having a baby. Mudear was so angry that she wouldn't talk to me for months, but she nor my Daddy put me out. And even though she didn't have much to say to me I knew she still loved me. She fed me everyday. She made sure I had three great meals a day. She showed her love through food. I disappointed her but she still loved me. Thank you Mudear. I love you.

Regina's Birthday Bash Seafood Boil

My birthday is May 22nd. I celebrate my birthday the whole month of May, but when my day comes the 22nd, I make sure I have lots of fun. I love the people in my life, so I call them and I say come over, bring something and let's hang out for my birthday. So for this year 2015 birthday, I had a ball... Yes I did... "Child" I had a seafood party hmmm. My favorite.

I told family and friend to bring all kind of great food...potato salad, some brought salmon—we put it on the grill—we had regular catfish, whiting—we fried that outside...Then we also had chicken, hot dogs and burgers for the kids. We had hot hushpuppies, hot water cornbread...One of my friend fix a large pot of gumbo hmmm. And I cooked (get ready) a foot tub of lobster, crab legs, shrimp, crawdads, corn on the cob, red potatoes, with cut up onion, boil crab seasoning, Old Bay seasoning...Lord have mercy it was good. Ok let me tell you what I did...

Ingredients

crab boil seasoning
Old Bay seasoning
1 stick butter
red potatoes
onion
corn
lobster
crab legs
shrimp
crawdads

Directions

Pour water halfway in pot or tub.
Put your crab seasoning with Old Bay and butter in the boiling water.
Cut your red potatoes in three or four pieces and cut an onion up.
Cut corn, small hand size, then put potatoes, onion and corn in water. Let it boil for 10 minutes. Put your lobster, crab legs, shrimp and crawdads in water and boil 10 minutes. Take all of it out of boiling water AND EAT.

Gina Mac Ooo Wee Seafood Gumbo

Ingredients

shrimp
crab meat and claws
smoked sausage
olive oil
1 stick butter
onion
green bell peppers
celery
okra
4 bags of gumbo mixed vegetables
flour
salt
pepper
water
sugar
gumbo file
cayenne pepper

Directions

Take shrimp and peel, clean crab meat out of shell, crab claws also.
Put all of this with smoked sausage into hot skillet.
Pour olive oil and butter in skillet.
Chop up onion, bell pepper and celery then add with shrimp, crab meat and smoked sausage to skillet.
Cook till done. Take all food out of skillet then pour flour slowly over in skillet, on top of the juice, olive oil and butter. Stir constantly.
Pour black pepper and salt, water and a little sugar over in skillet until it's brown gravy… Then set it to the side. Have a 1/2 pot of water with your three or four bags of gumbo vegetable mix boiling, cooking.

Then pour your shrimp, crab meat, crab claws, smoked sausage, celery, green bell peppers, okra and onion over in already cooking pot with vegetables. Now pour the gravy (roux) over in pot with everything else. Put in gumbo file to your taste and reduce heat to low simmer. Taste to your satisfaction with salt black pepper sugar cayenne pepper. You can make this with chicken and sausage or with no meat, still great.

Regina's Steak & Potato Soup on a Cold Day

I remember on the cold season, when the weather was 50s, 40s, 30s…Lord I don't like cold weather, but Mudear would go into the kitchen and create a delicious soup. It would warm our bodies and our hearts.

When I look back and truly think about it, we would slurp that soup. You could hear all of us just a-slurping. It was so good, and when I looked up at Mudear, she was smiling because she knew we were happy, warm and full.

When I make soup it's always when it's getting cold, and I call all my brothers and sisters, my grandkids, nieces, nephews and my friends to come get some or I'll take some to them. And when they eat it, I hear them slurp. I smile… I guess I'm like my Mama…

Ingredients

2 top select steaks
8 red potatoes
2 lbs. spring onions (chopped)
1 bunch of celery (chopped)
carrots (chopped)
1 bag frozen peas or 2 large bags frozen vegetables
1 can cream of celery
1 can cream of mushroom
1 can cream of potato
1 stick of butter (or more to taste)
1 container of garden vegetable cream cheese
1 cup of butternut squash
olive oil (to your desire)
balsamic vinegar
2 Tbsp Old Bay seasoning
1 Tbsp black pepper
pinch of salt
1/2 Tbsp chipotle and roasted garlic seasoning
meat tenderizer
3 Tbsp sugar

Directions

Take steak and rinse then cut the steak in very small cuts (cube). Cut up celery, onions, carrots and potatoes.
Pour olive oil, butter and balsamic vinegar into skillet.
Place cut up steaks, celery and onion in skillet with meat tenderizer.
Cook slowly and stir often.
Then get large pot and fill halfway with water.
Place cut up potatoes, carrots and peas into the water.
Add black pepper, Old Bay, salt, chipotle and roasted garlic seasoning and sugar.
Then pour in cream of celery, cream of mushroom, cream of potato and add butter.
Add butternut squash and cream cheese then put the steak, onion and celery in pot with all other ingredients.
Reduce heat to 4 and let it cook slow.
Cook for 30 more minutes.
Reduce to low and let simmer 10 more minutes.
Cut off and eat.

Regina's Creamy Chicken Vegetable Soup

Man, this is so hard for me. I've always loved people asking me, "Regina, how did you make this?" Or, "Oh! It's so good." And I would reply and say, "Awww…if I told you, I'd have to kill you." And we would all laugh, but still I wouldn't tell.

But because I love all of you and I promised Ann I would give up a few of my secrets, here I am doing it. So remember the main ingredient to this recipe is love. Make this for people you love and make this with love.

Ingredients

1 or 2 whole chickens
All these vegetables fresh or frozen (4 or more, your choice, but no canned vegetables):
- carrots
- celery
- corn
- okra
- peas
- red peppers

1 box chicken broth
1/2 pack of onion and chives cream cheese (about 3 Tbsp)
1/2 cup sugar
salt
black pepper
Old Bay seasoning (pinch)
1 large can Campbell's Cream of Chicken soup
1/2 stick of butter

Directions

Cook chicken in a large pot until done, then take the chicken out of the pot (do not throw away the leftover chicken broth).
Pull all the skin off of the chicken, shred chicken into pieces and place in a bowl.

Take the chicken broth from the box and pour a cup into the chicken broth leftover in the pot.

Take the fresh cut vegetables (or frozen bags) and pour into the chicken broth in the pot. Also, put butter plus the cream cheese, sugar, salt and pepper to taste and Old Bay seasoning then mix it all together.

Then put your shredded chicken back into the pot, pour cream of chicken into the pot and mix well, then let it simmer. Oh my goodness, it's delicious!

Regina's Story: New Year Eve Wild Meat Dinner

All year long Daddy's hobby was he love to hunt… and Daddy, his brother and friend would come together on Friday night, get their hound dogs and take off hunting, way out in the woods. Well Daddy would come home with something, deer, rabbit, raccoon, and Daddy would skin it and Mudear would clean it… Then she would prepare it, freeze it, and this would be what Daddy and Mudear would do. We had an old deep freezer that they stored the meat in. But those last three days of the year leading into New Year Eve and New Year Day morning, Mudear would take all that wild meat out of the freezer and start to prepare it, season, boil, bake, broil, cook all this meat along with candy yams, homemade bread, slaw, spaghetti, and much more. And at St. Mark Baptist Church, after we had shouted, sung, prayed and thank God for bringing us out of one year and into a new year, we had a meal… "Wild Meat Dinner." Now we also had chicken and ribs for the ones who did not want to eat the wild meat… Sorry, I couldn't eat the wild meat. I didn't want to eat "Bambi." Ain't nothing like praising the Lord, feeling his love, feeling the love of others, then eating together. I pray we all could do this one day…

Regina's Butt Pork Roast

I don't eat a lot of pork, but when I do…this is the way to go. It's so tender, it melts in your mouth. Listen, I can cook, I love cooking for my family and friends, and who knows one day I'll cook for my husband when he comes and gets me…until then, I'll just keep cooking for y'all. You are my family too. God bless you. Enjoy!

Ingredients

pork butt roast (as much or little as you like)
meat tenderizer
salt
black pepper
red pepper
1-2 bottles of BBQ sauce

Directions

Take a large pot of water and put it on the stovetop. Put your meat tenderizer, black pepper, red pepper and salt in the water and let it boil.
Take the pork butt roast and trim most of the fat off of the roast, and then puncture the meat repeatedly.
Put the pork roast in the pot of water with all of the seasonings in it, set the stove to 6 (medium/medium high) and let it cook for one hour.
Reduce heat to 4 on the temperature dial and let it cook for one hour.
Then reduce heat to low and let it stay at this temperature for another hour.
After reducing heat, pour 1 cup of BBQ sauce in the water and let cook for 30 minutes.
After cooking, take the meat out and shred it.
Top with the remaining BBQ sauce and serve.

Regina's Story: A Bag for the Road Full of Love

Ann, Deborah, Allen and I would go sing with this choir called the BC&M Mass Choir. We were young people from the ages of me being the youngest, 7 years old, to the age of 30's and 40's. Over 60 voices traveling all over the United States, singing praises to God, and loving it. BC&M stood for Baptist, Catholic and Methodist. No matter our religion we loved the Lord…

While traveling with them if we were going out of town (concert), Mudear would fry chicken, fix bologna sandwiches, send apples, cookies, soda, etc. so we could eat. She wanted to make sure we had good food, her food. She would give a hug, a kiss, a little money, make sure we had warm clothes, hats, gloves, and plenty of food to eat…

And the McCrary Sisters, man we still do that same thing. Especially if we are driving out of town to sing, food, food, food, ha ha ha some thing never change…

Regina's Quickie Hot Stuff

Ingredients

cream cheese
crab meat
jalapeño peppers
bacon
salt/black pepper (if you want)
toothpicks

Directions

Preheat oven to 350°.
Mix cream cheese and crab meat together.
Clean the seeds out of the jalapeño peppers.
Stuff inside of peppers with the cream cheese and crab meat.
Then take a strip of bacon and wrap around the jalapeño pepper.
Stick a toothpick in the bacon through the pepper.
Put them in the oven. Let the bacon cook on pepper.
When bacon on peppers is cooked enough for you, take out of oven let it cool down and eat.
Great for small get togethers or your own snack…hmmm.

Regina's Healthy Quickie

When I'm hungry but I don't want to eat heavy, this is what I do. It's simple y'all, but good and healthy...well it is to me!

Ingredients

2 cucumbers
2 tomatoes
1 onion
lemon juice
black pepper
Italian dressing

Directions

Slice cucumbers, tomatoes and onion.
Sprinkle lemon and black pepper on the vegetable mix then pour a small amount of Italian dressing on everything and eat, eat, eat!!

Regina's Bologna Sammich

Ingredients

thick bologna
cheddar cheese
tomato
lettuce
mayo
egg
two slices bread

Directions

Put bologna in hot skillet and flip it over from side to side.
Then fry an egg. Leave a small amount of yellow creamy.
You can toast bread or not.
Put mayo, lettuce and tomato on bread.
Place fried bologna on bread then fried egg and cheddar cheese.
Put bread together and get your lips ready to chow down because this is a great quick breakfast. Boy it's good.

Regina's Story: If There's a Kitchen in Heaven

You know I miss my Mudear, my Daddy, and Jesus knows my son Tony. Tony loved Mudear's cooking… So if there is a kitchen in heaven I know Mudear is teaching them how to cook… Angels all lined up, apron on.

The last few times Mudear was in the hospital and they brought her out of surgery… She was laying in the bed and still out of it, knocked out. She was shaking her arms like she was shaking salt and pepper on food. Then she said, while still knocked out, "Girl make sure you put enough salt and pepper on that chicken…" We all stopped what we were doing and just looked at her and started laughing. Mudear was cooking in her sleep… A few months later she was gone.

Mudear I know it's not a kitchen in heaven, but if it was… Mudear would be in heaven making everybody happy…hmmm I can smell it now… Cook Mudear cook… I love and miss you.

Freda's House

Freda's Story

Freda's Menu:

Freda's Pot Pie

Ann's Ground Beef & Turkey Meatloaf

Regina's Potatoes & Onions

Hot Water Cornbread

Regina's Hmmm Good Caramel Pie

Freda's Extras:

Freda's Party Dip

Freda's Tomato Artichoke Salad

Freda's Story

My mother Mudear was the best. I think everyone who had attended her funeral had eaten her food either at the house, or at church. Mudear, to me, was a great cook. She cooked for anyone and everybody. She would fix food and take to the law firm office where she worked and feed them all the time. They wanted her to open up her own restaurant, but she said that was too much work.

My Mom and Dad would go the store every Saturday for groceries. I would wonder why, but today I can understand. Tomorrow isn't promised to you and you stack up and save because you never know. Plus all of the mouths they had to feed!

After my mother's surgery, Daddy would go by himself and after his illness, I think I went more than anybody. One reason I don't like coupons to this day is because Mudear wore me out with coupons. I would be in line ready to pay, and then it seemed like we were in that line forever. Mudear had coupons for every item (so it seemed). That was part of her and why she enjoyed cooking for you and she loved every bit of it.

If Mudear didn't like something she would let you know. Nobody would have to say that "Mamie say this or that" cause she would tell you right then and there. Mudear was direct, told you off and then would love and feed you all in the same breath.

My mother was real and we don't have too many Mudear's left in this world today. I'm grateful for my parents. Because of who she was and how she taught me, and how my father helped me to be who I am today. So I appreciate my teaching. I love you Mudear and Daddy.

Freda's Pot Pie

Mudear would bring food home from school. They could do that back then. She would fix some stuff called goulash and it was fine. It had everything in it, but I thought I was fixing it one day and I was wrong. It turned out to be a pot pie. So I'm going to share it with you today. I think my Mom would be proud of me. It was so good!

Ingredients

chicken
pie shell
mixed vegetables (frozen is fine)
cream of mushroom soup
extra mushrooms (if desired)
dough

Directions

Preheat oven to 400°.
Combine chicken, mixed vegetables and cream of mushroom soup in the pie shell. Then cover the top with the dough. Or you can roll and make your dough the bottom and the top of the pie.
Place in oven and cook for 40 minutes or until golden brown.

Ann's Ground Beef & Turkey Meatloaf

I get tired of eating the same things cooked the same way, so I discovered that just changing some ingredients in a dish gives it just a little different taste. Sometimes it will make you think you're eating a different dish. Out of boredom I put beef and turkey together to make this meatloaf. Give it a try. I cooked it for two of my brothers and one of my sons and they loved it. Most of the time if it's halfway good, men will eat it because they don't want to hurt your feelings, but I believe they were honest when they said they liked it. Enjoy!

Ingredients

1 lb. ground beef
1 lb. ground turkey
1 onion
1 can Rotel tomatoes
1 can tomato sauce
1 egg (beaten)
salt
black pepper
seasoning salt

Directions

Preheat oven to 350°.
In a mixing bowl, mix ground beef and ground turkey.
Chop your onions and then add the onions to the meat mixture.
Add the beaten egg to the mixture, mixing in well.
Add your seasonings to taste (salt, black pepper and seasoning salt).
Add the Rotel tomatoes and mix well.
Add 1/4 cup of tomato sauce to the mixture and mix well.
With your hands, pat the meat mixture into a roll or whatever shape you want your meatloaf to be. Just make sure the meat mixture is firmly holding together.
Place into a cooking dish and bake for 45 minutes.
Then pour the rest of the tomato sauce over the meat mixture.
Cook another 15 to 25 minutes, depending on how fast your oven cooks.
This should feed about 4 if they are big eaters, or up to 6.

Regina's Potatoes & Onions

Ingredients

1 bag of red potatoes (sliced)
1 bag of onions (sliced)
water (about 4 oz.)
butter
olive oil
salt
black pepper
red pepper

Directions

Put butter and olive oil in skillet.
Let it heat up, then put the sliced potatoes in the skillet with sliced onion over them, adding a small amount of water.
Cook on medium high for 10 minutes.
Use salt and pepper to taste.
Cut temperature to low heat and let simmer, stirring every once in awhile.
When potatoes are soft and cooked enough for you, then you have potatoes and onions.
You can vary the amount you cook easily depending on serving size.

Ann's Hot Water Cornbread

Hot water cornbread is one of the first dishes that my mother taught me how to make, and it is one of the more simple things to cook. It is very important that the oil and water are hot. The water should be scalding hot. The quantity of ingredients you use depends on the amount of people you have to feed. Deborah will tell you how she makes her Hot Water Cornbread. It has the same ingredients, but I use different cooking techniques.

Ingredients

1 1/2 cups self-rising cornmeal
boiling hot water
cooking oil
bowl of cold water

Directions

Add boiling hot water to cornmeal. Mix it well and make sure your mixture is completely saturated because the hot water cooks the cornmeal. The cornmeal can't be too dry and not too wet. You should be able to make a soft patty.

What makes mine different from Deborah's is that I dip my hand in cold water, then I get a scoop of cornmeal mixture, then I pat it out and drop it into the hot oil. Add the cold water as you pat the mixture out. This gives the cornbread more of a crispy texture. But don't cook it too fast.

After the oil gets hot, cut it back on medium heat so the bread won't burn, and brown it on both sides.

I'm sure you will love it!

Deborah's Hot Water Cornbread

Ingredients

self-rising cornmeal
sugar
boiling hot water
cooking oil

Directions

Bring water to boil and slowly add dried cornmeal and sugar until mixture is firm enough to form.
Then make patties.
Make sure the oil is hot before applying the patties to the oil.
Measure ingredients according to how many people to serve (about 1 cup cornmeal to one tsp sugar).

Regina's Hmmm Good Caramel Pie

I'm very proud of this pie. I made many mistakes until I got it just like I want it, and now it's a winner. I only make this pie on special occasions. It's simple but takes a while to make. Important notice: This is not a diet pie…ha ha!!!

Ingredients

2 cans of condensed milk
graham cracker piecrust
Cool Whip

Directions

Take the two cans of condensed milk and put in a large pot of water (the cans, not just the condensed milk). Fill the pot full of water and let it boil for 3 hours.
Then take the cans out of the pot and let them sit for 5 minutes.
Very carefully open up the cans and pour the cooked milk into the piecrust and spread evenly, then place in the refrigerator for 2 hours.
After the pie is completely cooled off and ready to eat, spread Cool Whip all over it like icing and let set for 30 more minutes, and then eat.
Hmmm… I know it's good, enjoy!!
Please don't eat this and talk about losing weight…they don't go together.

Freda's Party Dip

When Mudear taught us how to cook, she taught us to taste as we went. You may have one teaspoon or one tablespoon of something that is required, but it probably needed more. We didn't do a lot of measuring, we just knew. I know a lot of people measure and some don't, but she taught us differently.

So some of these recipes you have to judge on the amount that you fix. My advice to you is to taste and add a little at a time. God Bless and I hope that you enjoy all that has been given. Thank you.

Ingredients

meat (ground beef or turkey)
American cheese
1 can of Rotel tomatoes (your choice of hot or mild)
chips

Directions

Cook the meat in a skillet and drain.
Add cheese until melted, cooking slowly.
Add the can of Rotel tomatoes and continue cooking until the cheese is fully melted in.
Let it cool and serve with tortilla chips or chips of your choice.

Freda's Tomato Artichoke Salad

I lived at home with my parents for a while during some of their sickness. I would go to the store for my parents, and take my Mom back and forth to the doctor's office.
Daddy would give me money and sometimes he would go and sit outside. If I didn't have enough money, I would have to run outside (mind you there were people behind me in line) and get the rest of the money. People would get so hot cause I had to hold up the line.

Mudear would like to play jokes. I took her to the doctor once and mind you, she had one of her legs amputated and she had a prosthetic leg. One of the doctors came in to take her pulse, but he had the wrong leg. Mudear was laughing when I realized what she was doing, and then I was cracking up too (at Vanderbilt they have two interns come in before the main doctor).

This went on for a while. The doctor went and got another doctor, and finally after this doctor found out the trick, he went and got another doctor to play the trick on him. Finally it stopped. The doctors would see her leg and it felt so real they thought it was her real leg. Mudear loved to laugh and plan jokes.

Ingredients

large plum tomatoes (quartered)
2 Tbsp basil pesto
2 Tbsp sherry vinegar
1 cup quartered artichoke hearts, drained
1/2 cup cheese croutons
2 cups baby spinach

Directions

Whisk pesto and vinegar in a salad bowl until well blended.
Add tomatoes, artichokes and croutons and toss until well blended.
Place spinach on platter and top with tomato mixture, and serve.

Deborah's House

Deborah's Story

Deborah's Menu:

Deborah's Baked Chicken

Deborah's Fried Cabbage

Freda's Fried Corn

Ann's Mashed Potatoes (with Cheese and/or Broccoli)

Regina's Green Beans

Tommy & Becky's Peanut Butter Pie

Deborah's Story: Play Cookin' to the Real Cookin'

Deborah's Story

I was very spoiled. I stayed up under my parents all the time, which gave me goody points. I would go to Sunday school on Sundays and stay in church all day. That was how I would have my Daddy all to myself, and I got a lot of attention from the women at the church.

I told on everybody all the time, and that really gave me favor with Mudear. Anything she wanted to know about my siblings I told it. I never got in trouble, because all I had to do was tell on somebody or cook something or clean up the house and they forgot all about what I did.

During the trying times of my life, Mudear was always there for me. There were times when I would do things that would hurt Mudear, and she never turned her back on me. There is no one like her, and she taught me a lot about cooking and loving. There were times when others would tell Mudear to put me out of her house, because of the things I would do, and she never would. She would tell me that I was her child and she would never put me out.

I wish she was here now to see the work we are doing, because I know she would be proud, and she would be glad that she didn't give up on me. I love her so much. The thought of her love helps me to make it through this life.

Deborah's Baked Chicken

Ingredients

chicken
salt
pepper
garlic powder
onion
water

Directions

Preheat oven to 350°.
Wash chicken and season with salt, pepper and garlic powder.
Cover bottom of baking pan with water.
Place chicken into baking pan.
Cut onion over top of chicken.
Cover pan and cook chicken until done. Enjoy!

Deborah's Fried Cabbage

Ingredients

1 cabbage
1/2 onion
1/2 bell pepper
1/2 stick of butter
Salt (season to taste)
Pepper (season to taste)

Directions

Cut up cabbage, onion and bell pepper and combine in a skillet.
Add butter, salt and pepper as desired.
Cook on medium heat until tender or how you prefer.

Freda's Fried Corn

Ingredients

ears of corn
sugar
3 Tbsp flour
1/4 cup oil
salt
pepper
1 cup water
1/4 cup butter

Directions

Shuck the corn and wash it.
Cut kernels of corn into skillet. Turn on medium heat.
Add water and oil. Let cook about 15 minutes.
Add salt, pepper, sugar and butter. Cook another 10 minutes.
Add flour for thickness.
Cook until desired thickness and tenderness.
Taste for desired flavor.
Yum yum eat it up!

Ann's Mashed Potatoes (with Cheese and/or Broccoli)

When my children were young, I would do whatever I could do to get them to eat vegetables. I had no problems getting them to eat green beans or greens, even spinach, corn or sweet potatoes because I would be sure it had enough flavor.

Sometimes our parents would overdo the flavors with too much butter or sugar or salt. So we try to be better than our parents and not add too much flavor. But there has to be a middle road. God gave us taste buds, so we could enjoy the flavors of the foods we eat.

Now back to the vegetables, I could not get my children to eat mashed potatoes. They would take one or two bites and that was it. So this is my hint for mashed potatoes – add cheddar cheese. Most children love cheese and you will enjoy it too, and make sure it has a little flavor. For broccoli—flavor it up and add just a little more butter.

Ingredients

potatoes (4 or more)
broccoli (1 package frozen)
1 cup milk
1/2 stick butter
salt
pepper
cheese

Directions

Peel potatoes and cut them in medium size.
Boil until soft then drain water off potatoes.
Mash potatoes. Add butter, salt, pepper and half the milk.
Cook broccoli in separate pan. Drain water.
Add broccoli and cheese to potatoes.
Add other half of milk and turn on low heat. Stir frequently.
After potatoes heat up, turn off, and watch your children love them.

Regina's Green Beans—Watch Out Now!

Now my family would really trip on me about this one... I would watch my momma (Mudear) pick and clean (wash in the kitchen sink) her green beans. So, I really love going to the Farmer's Market and getting fresh green beans.

How funny that sounds to even me...going out to pick fresh green beans, the girl who doesn't really cook a lot! But baby when I make my mind up to cook...a sister throw down! Enjoy.

Ingredients

fresh green beans
5 or 6 small red potatoes
1 leg smoked turkey
1 onion (optional)
Old Bay seasoning (to taste)
salt
pepper
red pepper (pinch)
2 tbsp of sugar
1 1/2 cup of Italian dressing

Directions

Take a large pot, put 1/2 pot of water and put the smoked turkey leg into the pot.
Add seasoning, salt, pepper, sugar and chopped up onion into the pot.
Let it all boil, then cut up the red potatoes and pick and clean the fresh green beans.
As everything is boiling, put green beans and red potatoes into the pot.
Take the Italian dressing and pour into the pot and let it all cook.
After 20 minutes of boiling, slowly start to decrease heat down to simmer.
Let cook and simmer for 45 minutes.

Tommy & Becky's (Regina's friends) Peanut Butter Pie

My best friend Becky and Tommy gave me this wonderful recipe. Whenever I go to Austin, Texas, where they live, I'm always asking Tommy to make this pie. And man it is delicious. Thanks Tommy and Becky.

Ingredients

2/3 cup sugar
3 Tbsp cornstarch
1/4 tsp salt
2 1/2 cups evaporated milk
2 egg yolks (lightly beaten)
1/2 cup peanut butter
1 tsp vanilla extract
graham cracker piecrust

Directions

Combine sugar, cornstarch and salt in saucepan.
Slowly stir in evaporated milk.
Cook over medium heat until thick and bubbly.
Gradually stir one quarter of hot mixture into beaten egg yolks. Add this to remaining mixture.
Cook, stirring with wire whisk, for 3 minutes.
Remove from heat.
Add peanut butter and vanilla then stir until smooth.
Pour into piecrust and chill for 3 hours.
Top with whipped cream.

Deborah's Story: Play Cookin' to the Real Cookin'

I always wanted to cook like Mudear. I watched her cooking everyday, so I would go outside and play like I was Mudear and play cook outside.

I would get leaves off the trees for my turnip greens. The tree bark would be my BBQ ribs. Little dandelions for eggs…mud and sugar for pie…and a flower that when you mashed or cut it up, it looked slimy, that was my okra.

Then I would call Ricky, Regina and Freda to come eat. And sometimes they would take a bite, especially the pie.

I would always pretend to cook until I actually start cooking for real. Then I would cook sometimes dinner, because Mudear worked so hard, I would help her out by cooking fried chicken, peas, potatoes, or mash potatoes.

That's how I learned to cook so good. Mudear would tell me what I needed to do if something wasn't right.

But also my cooking got me favor. I cleaned the kitchen, cook, and I can see Mudear smiling now. I played until I got it right.

Sundays at the McCrary's

Regina's Story: Funny Sunday Morning Memory

Regina's Fried Apples

Ann's Pork Chops & Gravy

Regina's Story: Funny Sunday Morning Memory

Every Sunday morning Mudear would cook breakfast. Then she would start cooking her Sunday dinner, so when we leave church service, we come home and dinner would be ready.

So Mudear had her gospel music on and she was singing, praising the Lord and cooking. Every once in awhile I'd hear Mudear shout "Hal-le-lu-jah, yes Lord yes…"

I hear Mudear singing louder then I came into the kitchen. I was fixing me a plate of breakfast food while Mudear was cooking, singing and praising the Lord. I looked at Mudear and she had tears in her eyes. I noticed she was really getting happy (a term for shouting). I also noticed that Mudear had a bag of flour in her hand. She looked at me, tears streaming down her face while smiling. Her eyes got big and she went in (shouting). Flour went everywhere, all over me. I ran out of the kitchen.

Well let me just say when the Holy Spirit got through with Mudear, and I looked back in the kitchen, flour was everywhere—Mudear's hair, her clothes, the walls, absolutely everywhere—and she looked at me with this giant smile on her face and said, "Ain't God good…come on and eat." We cleaned up the flour and Mudear started back cooking, singing, what a memory.

Sunday morning was fried apples, homemade biscuits, rice, pork chops and gravy, scrambled eggs… Baby we thought we were rich. Any meal Mudear cooked was fit for a king or queen. She had that gift, that talent, that touch—love.

Regina's Fried Apples

Ingredients

bag of red cooking apples (for serving 6 or more)
nutmeg
vanilla extract
butter
sugar
cinnamon

Directions

Slice up apple. Get rid of the core of apple.
Peel some apple. Also leave a few peelings.
Get skillet heat medium high.
Melt butter, put in apples then sugar, nutmeg, cinnamon and vanilla extract (all to your taste).
Cook until apples are soft enough for you.
Take off heat, let apples simmer down, and eat.

Ann's Pork Chops & Gravy

Ingredients

pork chops
salt
pepper
cooking oil
flour
water

Directions

Put your oil in skillet and heat on medium high.
Season pork chops with salt and pepper.
Cover both sides of chops with flour and place into hot skillet—don't cook too fast!
Lower heat to medium and brown chops on both sides.
When chops are done, take them out of the skillet.
Pour most of the oil out, leaving only a small amount in the skillet.
Sprinkle flour into the oil and let it cook. The oil and flour will cook to a brown color.
Stir the oil and flour and slowly add water. This is a judgment call because you don't want the gravy to be too thick.
Add the chops back into the skillet.
Cover and simmer for a few minutes more. Watch that the gravy doesn't get too thick.
Onions can be added if desired. Enjoy!

Holidays at the McCrary's

Regina's Holiday Story

Thanksgiving and Christmas Menu:

Regina's Ham for Christmas

McCrary Holiday Turkey & Dressing

Cisco's Country Skillet Bread

Eben & Cathy's Cornbread Dressing

Ann's Potato Salad

Ann's Pineapple Sweet Potatoes

Ann's Stuffed Eggs

Deborah's Cheesy Macaroni & Cheese

Freda's Collard Greens

Ann's Corn Pudding

Ann's Baked Cherry Cheese Pie

Ann's Chess Pie

Cathy's Fudge

Regina's Holiday Story

When we were young Mudear would cook Thanksgiving and Christmas dinner. Now that I look back that was a lot of cooking… And Mudear cooked it all. We had ham, turkey and dressing, sweet potatoes with marshmallows, green beans, turnip greens, potato salad, corn, mac and cheese, squash casserole, homemade rolls, cucumbers and onion marinated in vinegar, cakes, chess pie, banana pudding, sweet tea, etc. And Mudear year after year cooked it all and loved it… One day I pray to be just half the woman she was. Now on Thanksgiving and Christmas we make up a menu, and we all pick what we're cooking and we meet at the family home and celebrate. I'm the ham girl…cakes, pies and sometimes green beans, corn…

After everybody finished eating Christmas dinner, we all would go outside on the front porch. We'd put on our coats, boots, caps and scarves, and stand on the front porch—and it would be cold—and sing, sing, sing from the youngest to the oldest McCrary. And when Mudear and Daddy was alive it would be all of us. IT WAS GLORIOUS… I remember looking at Mudear and Daddy while we were all singing and they would smile with LOVE AND HEARTFELT JOY, thanking GOD for their family and blessing us. They would stand next to each other and hold hands and look at the family. We still sing on Christmas Day, out on the front porch after we finish eating, and even though Daddy and Mudear are not here, WE CAN STILL FEEL THEIR SPIRIT. I CAN, IN MY SPIRITUAL EYES, SEE MUDEAR AND DADDY ON THE PORCH STILL SMILING AT ALL OF US, AND IN MY HEART I ALWAYS SAY MERRY CHRISTMAS MUDEAR AND DADDY.

Regina's Ham for Christmas

Ingredients

28-32 lb. ham
brown sugar
meat tenderizer
honey
Coca Cola
cinnamon sticks
2 cans pineapple (1 each circles and crushed)

Directions

Preheat oven to 450°.
Clean all the extra fat off ham.
Have a big knife to stab ham all over and a very large baking pan or large disposable pan. After cleaning off extra fat from ham, take a large knife and stab ham all over. Put ham in pan.
Mix cola, meat tenderizer, juice from pineapple, honey and brown sugar all together. Pour all over ham. Cover ham with aluminum foil and put in oven.
After 1 hour, stick cinnamon sticks in ham and place pineapple circles on cinnamon sticks.
Pour a little crushed pineapple over ham and pull some of the juice you poured on the ham off the ham. Then pour back on again every hour.
Bake for 3 hours at 450°. Lower the oven heat after third hour, down to 300°.
Pour more honey on ham and bake one more hour then cut off oven.
You just made a honey baked ham for any time, but I only cook this for Thanksgiving and Christmas.

McCrary Holiday Turkey & Dressing

Ingredients

turkey
salt
pepper
seasoning salt
country skillet bread (recipe on next page)
4 pieces of toast
onion
celery
sage

Directions

Turkey
Preheat oven to 350°. Thaw turkey if frozen.
Wash turkey. Remove the sacks of neck, liver and gizzard from the turkey.
Season turkey with salt, pepper and seasoning salt.
Place turkey in a roasting pan. Cover and cook according to size (about 20 minutes per pound for a defrosted turkey or 10 to 15 minutes per pound for fresh).
Save the broth from the turkey.

Dressing
Crumble the country skillet bread and pieces of toast into a baking dish.
Dice onion and celery into a skillet or pot. Add turkey broth and season to taste with salt, pepper and sage. Cook until tender.
Mix all ingredients well, until softened and wet but not too wet.
Put baking dish in oven until light brown on top.

Cisco's (Freda's husband) Country Skillet Bread

I'm the baby of the family and my mother was the best cook to me than anyone in the world. That's just how good her cooking was. She could cook anything.

I can't cook hot water cornbread, skillet bread or any other kind of bread. I always wanted to know how to cook cornbread, but I was told "you're gonna get burnt," and that stayed with me. Even when I was older and tried to fix it, I did get burned over and over.

I still kept right on, but I wasn't burning myself, I just didn't know what I was doing and still can't get it right.

But now I'm married and all of my worries are over. When the bread needs to be fixed, my husband Cisco can fit hot water cornbread, skillet bread and all the other kinds of bread. He says "you gotta learn," and I replied as long as you're here, I will love you and you do the bread. So here you go. Cisco's bread is so good it makes you wanna smack your Momma (or not!).

Ingredients

1/2 bag of self-rising cornmeal
2 eggs
1 cup sugar
2 cups milk
1/2 cup oil
Salt (optional)

Directions

Preheat the oven to 350° and put the skillet in the oven, greased with hot oil.
Pour the cornmeal into a bowl and add eggs, milk and sugar. Mix the oil in last, but it must be hot (very hot). Leave in the oven for 20-25 minutes.
Spread butter or margarine on top and then let cool for 5-10 minutes.
Serve. (Use less or more ingredients accordingly.)

Eben & Cathy's (Regina's friends) Cornbread Dressing

Eben and Cathy have for years been family to me and they have been in my corner. My three dogs look to Eben as their Daddy (for real).

One Thanksgiving, we had a big family dinner and Eben made his dressing. Baby, everybody ate it all. So my family is the kind that if they love your cooking they ask you to fix it all the time. I love Eben and Cathy so much. Thanks for being a part of our family.

Ingredients

3 10-inch pans of cornbread
2 sleeves saltine crackers
1/2 loaf wheat or white bread
2 onions (medium, chopped)
6 celery stalks, finely chopped
2 tsp garlic powder
salt
black pepper
sage
6-10 cups of chicken broth (homemade or boxed/canned)

Directions

Preheat oven to 375°.
Break up cornbread, crush crackers and tear bread into small pieces. Then put into a large aluminum pan.
Apply onion and celery and some of the chicken broth, mash together (a potato masher works best).
Continue applying the broth along with the spices (salt, pepper and sage to taste).
You will want the dressing to be fairly moist.
Bake for 30 minutes or until the top is brown.
Serves 20. Enjoy!

Ann's Potato Salad

The amount of potatoes you use will depend on how many people you have to feed. When I make potato salad for our family, I use a whole sack of potatoes and one dozen eggs. So I will give you the ingredients and directions and you will have to determine how much to prepare.

Ingredients

potatoes
eggs
onion
celery
bell pepper
1 Tbsp mustard
sweet pickle relish
1/2 cup salad dressing
salt
pepper
1 tsp vinegar
1 Tbsp sugar

Directions

Boil potatoes and eggs. Don't let potatoes get mushy.
When eggs are boiled, pour the hot water off the eggs.
Shake the pot so the eggs will crack easily.
Cover eggs with cold water and add salt. Let eggs cool then peel.
Dice potatoes, eggs, onions, celery and bell peppers, and put in a large bowl.
Add sweet pickles, salt, pepper, vinegar and sugar, and mix ingredients.
Add mustard and salad dressing.
Mix well. You can add more salad dressing if it is too stiff, but don't get it too wet.

Ann's Pineapple Sweet Potatoes

When I was a little girl, I discovered that I love butter, not margarine, but butter. I still love butter to this day. My grandmother, who we called Mama, made her own butter. They had to hide the butter from me because I would always get in the butter. I guess it was my mission to always find it.

On one occasion that I vividly remember, I found the butter again in a bucket and no one discovered me missing for awhile. This gave me time to not just taste the butter, but to really discover the butter. So I discovered that butter made my skin feel soft, so I rubbed it all over my feet, arms, legs and face. Then I discovered that butter made my hair slick down, so I put the butter all through my hair and my hair was slick to my head. I was sitting on the floor and I remember looking up and a bunch of grown-ups were looking down at me. Some were frowning or shaking their heads, or laughing. But I never got in the butter after that.

When I fix sweet potatoes or pies during the holidays, I use plenty of butter—not margarine. Since we are more health conscious now, I only fix this on holidays or special occasions.

Ingredients

5 large sweet potatoes
2 sticks butter
2 cups sugar
1-2 cans crushed pineapple
nutmeg
all spice
ginger
1-2 bags of marshmallows

Directions

Preheat oven to 350°.
Boil the sweet potatoes until completely tender then mash them in a large baking pan.
Melt butter and add to sweet potatoes.
Add sugar slowly (taste to your desired sweetness).

Add all the spices (nutmeg, all spice and ginger) to taste.

After ingredients are completely mixed, add pineapples, 1 can or both if you desire.

Mix all ingredients and put into oven.

Cook 40 minutes—don't let the sweet potatoes get too dry.

Take the pan out of the oven and let sit for about 15 minutes.

Add marshmallows to the top and cook on 400° until the marshmallows are golden brown. Enjoy!

(This will feed a whole lot of people!)

Ann's Stuffed Eggs

Ingredients

eggs
salt
pepper
sweet pickle relish
mustard
salad dressing

Directions

Boil eggs well done, about 15 to 20 minutes.
When eggs are boiled, pour the hot water off the eggs.
Shake the pot so the eggs will crack easily.
Cover eggs with cold water and add salt.
Let stand for at least 10 minutes.
Peel eggs and cut in half.
Remove the yellow and put in mixing bowl.
Place the white of the eggs on a dish or plate.
Smash the yolk or yellow, making sure there are no lumps.
Add salt and pepper, then mix.
Add sweet pickle and mix.
Add 1 tsp mustard and mix.
Add salad dressing. Make sure the texture is not to dry or too wet.
Spoon the yolk mixture into the egg white, and you have yourself a good stuffed egg.

Deborah's Cheesy Macaroni & Cheese

Ingredients

1 box of macaroni noodles
1 package Velveeta cheese
1/2 cup milk
1 small package mozzarella cheese

Directions

Preheat oven to 350°.
Boil noodles.
Melt Velveeta with milk (microwave or in a sauce pan).
In a large baking pan, add cheese sauce and noodles to the pan and mix together.
Add mozzarella cheese and cook in oven until brown on top.

Freda's Collard Greens

My mom could cook turnip greens like nobody else. We would taste other people's greens and wonder what happened. I think we were spoiled when it came down to food.

When I was a little girl, there was a man in the neighborhood that came and he had all kinds of vegetables, fruits and cooking meats. When he got on your street he would blow the horn and yell, "Market man!" We would run and yell, "The market man is outside." So all of the kids and some of the parents in the neighborhood would go out and purchase all kinds of stuff. He would sit there for hours until everybody got what they wanted. This happened for some time, until crime got bad in the neighborhood.

My mom would get her greens from the market man. She would get sweet potatoes, tomatoes, green beans and sometimes her meat. Before she died, we would go the Farmer's Market to get the things that we would get from the truck or Kroger. My mother was so funny. If she didn't go inside of the store with you and she forgot to tell you to get something, somebody would come up to you and say, "Your Momma said to pick up (whatever it was that she forgot to get)." She would find anybody walking by and tell them what you were wearing and your name. This happened all of the time.

I really miss my Mom. She was so real and I can put love into my food like she did. Thanks Mudear.

Ingredients

collard greens
1 cup olive oil (or cooking oil)
1 onion (chopped)
salt
smoked turkey or smoked pork (optional)

Directions

In a large pot, boil water and add salt, onion, meat of your choice and the oil. How much salt, onions, meat and oil you use will depend on how many greens you want to cook. Thoroughly wash the greens until all of the dirt is removed. You can cut or pull the stems and I suggest you leave some of the stem.

Put the greens into the boiling water and constantly stir, watching the pot to make sure it doesn't overflow.

After each batch that you put in the pot, cook it down a little adding salt accordingly.

Ann's Corn Pudding

Corn is also one of my favorite foods. My mother made some of the best corn pudding ever. When Mudear passed away, I thought this recipe was gone with her. But one day while talking to my daughter, she told me that Mudear gave the recipe to her husband, Steve. Mudear loved Steve. She never let anyone in her kitchen while she was cooking, unless you were helping her. But I found out that she would let Steve (who is a very good cook) sit in her kitchen while she cooked, and she gave him several recipes. So here is Mudear's Corn Pudding.

Ingredients

2 cans yellow corn
1 bell pepper
1 medium onion chopped
4 Tbsp of sliced pimentos
3 eggs
1 cup sugar
1 cup milk
1/2 cup flour
1/2 stick unsalted butter
Salt and pepper to taste

Directions

Preheat oven to 350° for 10 minutes.
Mix all the ingredients and bake for 45 minutes.

Ann's Baked Cherry Cheese Pie

Ingredients

2 packages cream cheese
2 eggs
3/4 to 1 cup sugar
1 can cherry pie filling
1/4 cup lemon juice
1 tsp vanilla extract
1 graham cracker piecrust

Directions

Preheat oven to 350°.
In a mixing bowl, mash the cream cheese until it is smooth.
Add sugar and mix well.
Add eggs and mix well.
Add lemon juice and mix well.
Add vanilla and mix all ingredients.
Put into the piecrust.
Cook for 15 minutes.
If the middle does not feel firm, cook for another 5 minutes.
Take pie out and let it cool.
Add cherry pie filling on top.
Cover and put in the refrigerator until it's time to eat it up.

Ann's Chess Pie

Ingredients

1 stick butter
1 1/2 cups sugar
1 Tbsp all-purpose flour
1 Tbsp vinegar
1 Tbsp cornmeal
pinch salt
4 eggs (beaten)
2 Tbsp vanilla extract

Directions

Preheat oven to 425°.
In saucepan on medium heat, melt butter.
Add sugar then stir in all-purpose flour, vinegar, cornmeal and salt.
Mix in the beaten eggs and stir well.
Remove from heat.
Cool a little bit before adding vanilla extract.
Bake at 425° degrees for 10 minutes.
Turn oven to 350° and bake for 50 more minutes or until done, when you can poke a butter knife in middle of pie and it comes out clean.

Cathy's (Regina's friend) Fudge (This is great for a Christmas gift or snack)

Hey Cathy is one of my best friends (I've got four). We're sisters, but baby my grandkids (Aliyah and Dashean) love her. They crave Cathy's fudge like crazy. Every Christmas, Thanksgiving and Easter, Fourth of July, Labor Day, Memorial Day, my birthday, your birthday, everybody's birthday!

Aliyah and Dashean couldn't find enough reasons to ask Cathy to make fudge. Thank you Cathy for loving and making me and my grandchildren happy. We love ya!

Ingredients

1 package of semi-sweet chocolate chips
1/2 cup of marshmallow cream
2/3 cup evaporated milk
1 1/2 sticks of butter
3 cups of sugar
1/2 tsp vanilla extract

Directions

Combine sugar, milk and butter in a heavy saucepan.
Heat to boiling, stirring constantly for 5 minutes over medium heat or until the mixture comes to a soft boil stage.
Remove from heat. Stir until well blended.
Pour into a greased 13x9x2-inch pan and let cool.
Makes 3 pounds…so good!!

As you look at this picture, everybody is still not here. Some are missing, some are out of town, some have passed on, but we still get together, and love, laugh, sing, dance, tell jokes, cook and eat…

We look forward to coming together, being a family, caring for each other. That's the way Mudear and Daddy would have it…

Now that you have read this book, you've become a member of our family. We love and care about you. God bless you.

-McCrary Sisters

McCrary Cooking and Table Do's and Don'ts:

1. Please wash your hands. If you cough or sneeze into your hand, wash your hands again.

2. Do not touch your nose while cooking.

3. Try to use the bathroom before you go into the kitchen. If you scratch your hair, wash your hands. If you pick your nose, wash your hands.

At the table:

1. Please do not blow your nose at the table. It can make some people sick to their stomach to see or hear a person blow their nose at the table.

2. Please don't stand over people sitting at the table with their food on the table. Why, you ask? Because as you talk, you could inadvertently spit onto someone's food. Please stand back a little.

3. Be careful when talking while sitting next to someone who is eating for the same reason as when you are standing over people who are eating.

4. Please ask before you pick out of someone else plate. And if you want to taste something off of someone plate, please use clean utensils.

About the McCrary Sisters

Dynamic, powerful and thrilling are just a few words to describe the McCrary Sisters' live performances. Steeped in tight soulful harmonies, the Sisters will have the audience dancing in the aisles, celebrating life with words of hope and love.

The McCrary Sisters (Ann, Deborah, Regina and Alfreda) are the daughters of the late Rev. Samuel McCrary—one of the original members of the legendary gospel quartet The Fairfield Four. The daughters were raised in harmony, singing at home and at their father's church, but word soon spread of their individual accomplished voices and each began sharing the family vocal legacy as solo artists with a wide range of performers to include Bob Dylan, Elvis, Isaac Hayes and Stevie Wonder.

In 2011, the Sisters officially formed their own group, the McCrary Sisters, and have recorded or performed with The Black Keys, Martina McBride, Eric Church, Patty Griffin, Buddy Miller, Jonny Lang, Robert Randolph, The Winans, Donnie McClurkin, *Nashville*'s Jonathan Jackson, Mike Farris and many more. They have been featured on *Bobby Jones Gospel* and TBN's *Jason Crabb Show*.

Ann is the oldest sister in a family of eight children and is the backbone of the group. She traveled and sang with The Fairfield Four from the age of 3 until she was 6. Soon after, she worked with various gospel groups on the weekends until she began singing and traveling with the BC&M Mass Choir (Baptist, Catholic, and Methodist) as one of their soloists. As a strong lead vocalist, Ann has performed with the who's who of contemporary gospel music, including The Winans, Donnie McClurkin, Yolanda Adams, and many more. Ann was also a member of Bobby Jones's Nashville Super Choir for 12 years.

Regina is a true show woman and her tambourine playing skills are legendary. She began her singing career traveling with the BC&M Mass Choir as one of the soloists at the age of 7, and was known throughout the choir's travels for singing/recording "I Made A Vow" (the recording was nominated for a Grammy). With an award-winning voice, Regina toured and performed for six years with the legendary songwriter Bob Dylan. She recorded three albums with Dylan: *Slow Train Coming*, *Saved*, and *Shot of Love*, also performed with Elvis and Stevie Wonder, and has sung with Bobby Jones and The New Life Singers, and The Nashville Super Choir.

Deborah is the deep, low voice of the group. She also has been singing her whole life, and in her early teens she sang in the multi-Grammy-nominated BC&M Mass Choir, and has performed "Everything Is Beautiful" with Ray Stevens, sang with Elvis at Madison Square Garden, and performed with Isaac Hayes on Dinah Shore's TV show. Deborah spent most of her adult life working as a nurse, but now focuses on singing with her sisters.

Alfreda rarely sang with her sisters until the group formed, but was still filling rooms with her soulful soprano. She dedicated much of her time singing and preaching in the music ministry industry with her husband Narcisco Lee, at the Old Happy Day Church. Alfreda's notes will stop an audience and render them speechless. Alfreda has joined her sisters' singing sessions for Martina McBride, The Black Keys, Dr. John and many others. As the youngest sister of the group, she brings a joyful energy to every performance.

While working with Bob Dylan, Regina McCrary met Dr. John. In 2012, the Sisters performed with Dr. John and Dan Auerbach of The Black Keys to promote Dr. John's Grammy Award-winning album *Locked Down*, which featured them as background vocalists.

Recent performance highlights include the 2015, 2014 and 2013 Americana Music Awards backing Don Henley, Loretta Lynn, Jackson Browne, Rosanne Cash and working with celebrity band members Don Was, Ry Cooder, Buddy Miller and many more. The McCrary Sisters were also featured in live musical tributes to Jerry Garcia, Gregg Allman, Lynyrd Skynyrd, Dr. John and Mavis Staples. Upcoming shows include performing at the White House in Washington D.C., Sandy Beaches Cruise with Delbert McClinton and Friends, and tours in the U.K/Scotland and Ireland.

The McCrary Sisters' new CD *Let's Go*, released in spring 2015, was produced by Buddy Miller and features a song with The Fairfield Four. The McCrary Sisters and The Fairfield Four also shared the stage during the taping of the All-Star PBS Pledge Special, *Rock My Soul: A Celebration of the Gospel Quartet*. This national PBS special featured guest artists Lee Ann Womack, Buddy Miller, Amos Lee, Lucinda Williams and Van Hunt.

The new album *Let's Go* and the National PBS Pledge Special DVD *Rock My Soul* join the 2011 CD release *Our Journey* and 2013's *All The Way* (available though McC RECORDS/THIRTY TIGERS).

www.mccrarysisters.com

www.facebook.com/mccrarysisters

www.twitter.com/mccrarysisters

Made in the USA
Columbia, SC
16 October 2024